Animal

Trails

Poems about Animals

by Diana Smit

ISBN:1507797133

Table of Contents

The Penguin

Waiting for some tasty fish
    The penguin flaps his wings.
All winter long his only wish
    Is to eat what mother brings.

Little Brown Bear

Little brown bear, by the stream
 Splashing, making swishes.
Little brown bear, come and see
 Mother catching fishes.
Little brown bear, come and eat
 The fishes are delicious!

The Sea Turtle

Slowly, the sea turtle digs a nest
On a stretch of soft, warm sand.
And when she's laid one hundred eggs
She crawls away as planned.
She does not turn or care to see
How her young survive.
Instead, she heads to the ocean
And takes a deep-sea dive.

Harvest Mice

In a field of golden wheat
Tiny harvest mice meet.
Following mother's silent feet
They search for food to eat.

A Snake's Love

Shivering through the chilly nights
To keep her offspring warm,
She watches from the brooding nest
Through every kind of storm.
Tenderly, she wraps herself around
Her young so they will live.
Protecting them with the fiercest love
Only a mother can give.
For days she does not leave her charge
Her passion runs deep.
And creatures daren't disturb her
Though it seems she's fast asleep.
Then as the eggs begin to hatch
Green Python slinks away.
It's time to build another nest
Her work is done today.

The Lion Cub

He stalks, then pounces
On a beetle small.
He lurks, then prances
Like a bouncing ball.

He tucks, then lunges
As brother moves away.
He swats and wrestles
In grassy plains all day.
He sleeps, then wakes
When Mother brings the kill.
He stops, then waits
Till Father eats his fill!

Polar Bear Cub

Polar bear, deep inside your cave,
Though, the sun is not yet showing.
Mother will be your warmth and light
When winter winds are blowing.

The Pippit Song

He's a lively little fellow
And sings a happy song
In his brown feather coat
Only six inches long.
Though bashful and shy
He likes to run and hop
In high, grassy places
And can't seem to stop.
And when he sits upon a rock
Or a tall shady tree
He wags his little tail
And sings merrily.

The Call of the Penguin

Sound the royal trumpets.
Get ready for a feast.
Send out the invitations
To the greatest and the least.
It's time for celebrations.
Yes, it's a happy day!
Gather round every chick.
Don't dawdle or delay.
For Papa has come home from sea
And brought a tasty snack.
So open up your hungry beaks,
Cause Papa has come back!

The Flatfish Jamboree

In the deep, muddy waters at the bottom of the sea
Lives a funny little fish that is flat as could be.

With eyes a bulging on the top of his flat head
He watches out for danger from his little sandy bed.

He's not at all like other fish with fins to move about.
He's flat like a pancake and wears a funny pout.

While other fish are sleeping in their beds in the sea,
The flatfish come together for a secret jamboree.

All night they dance in concert and do the jitterbug,
Gliding through the waters like a magic carpet rug.

Then as the sun begins to shine the flatfish find their beds,
And tuck themselves into the sand like errant sleepyheads.

My Kitten

My kitten strikes the air
And arc's his fluffy back.
He's a ball of fluff commotion
With a mindset to attack.

Running in random circles
He takes a giant leap
On things imaginary,
On things that like to creep.

Seeing me, he starts to purr,
And climbs into my lap.
Then curls into a snail like ball
And takes a little nap.

The Spider-ling

Soar spider-ling, soar.
Leave your nursery bed.
Climb the tallest blade of grass
And spin your silky thread.
Feel the breeze—catch the wind,
Then sail far, far and away.
To a journey that's ahead of you
In a land of endless play.

A Beetle's Point of View

Let's imagine for a moment
From a bugs point of view,
You were changed into a beetle
Instead of being you.

Just imagine if you could
How strange you would feel,
If you lived inside the body
Of a small tank of steel.

Now imagine what you'd eat
In this new circumstance.
You would munch on tiny aphids
That ruined garden plants.

Let's imagine for a moment
A giant looked down from the sky on you.
Does it change your perspective,
Of a beetles point of view.

Little Rabbit

Little rabbit, small and helpless
Hairless, deaf and blind
Wrapped up snug in a grassy nest
So your foes can't find.

Soon your tiny hairless ears
Will help you hear each sound.
Soon your tiny legs will grow
To help you leap around.

Little rabbit soft and white
Your life has just begun.
Little rabbit soon you'll know
You were born to leap and run.

The Canadian Goose

Behold in the sky
The Canadian goose,
Wears a fine tux
Of chocolate mousse.
With matching attire
His friends honk too,
Bowing their long necks
And say, how are you!
After greeting each other
They honk their goodbyes
And with a flap of their wings
Soar through the skies.

My Budgie

My sweet feathery blue
Confined to a cage,
Sings to an audience
Inside a wire stage.
All day the songs continue,
As if he never heard
That songs are required
From a little caged bird!

The Hawk

One morning I passed by a hawk,
He was perched high up in a tree.
Ever so regal he ignored me.
It was glorious to see.

I watched his tail unfold like a fan.
He spread his wings on his back.
And with eyes like pools of black,
No confidence did he lack.

Suddenly, he unleashed his strength.
And he soared down from the skies.
And with his built in camera eyes,
He caught a mouse by surprise.

Two Little Frogs

Two little frogs in a barrel of cream
Were swimming with all their might.
One stopped swimming and so he sank
Into the barrel, out of sight.

The second little frog said to himself,
"A miracle might pass my way."
So he churned his legs till' butter was formed
Then jumped out to freedom that day.

The Sloth

The sloth is a thoughtful fellow
And moves persistently slow.
To arrive on time it matters not
He's in no hurry to go.

It may take the sloth a day or two,
To reach the end of the street.
It appears that he is thinking
Of where to place his feet.

The sloth doesn't mind what others say.
He's on a special crusade.
Resting in treetops, singing all day
Thankful is how he's made!

The Wiggly Worm

Out from the earth, damp and firm
Pops a wiggly, little brown worm.
He wiggles and squiggles and crawls about
Eating up brown dirt is a daily workout.

The little brown worm has no head or end
And no little arms or legs to bend.
He never has a reason to look in the skies
Cause he has no face or two little eyes.

The rain and the sun is the worms worst fear.
It dries up his skin and wets his ear.
Birds and fish will eat him for a treat
Why can't they find something else to eat!

Bee Party

When leaves fall, bees are busy.

They are buzzing everywhere.

They're having an autumn party.

So don't disturb them there.

But if you dare to go outdoors

When bees will buzz about,

Wear a hat for goodness sakes

Or they could knock you out.

The Ant's Shopping Bag

When the ant goes shopping
There's no time for stopping
Or playing a game a tag.
The ant's on a mission
And paid a commission
To fill her shopping bag!

Her shopping bag is a chunk of leaf
And it's the ant's firm belief
To recycle and not waste time.
And because she loves honey
She finds it quite funny
To be included in this rhyme!

When shopping day's complete
It's really kind of neat
To watch the ant begin to munch
On her leafy shopping bag.
Waving it proudly like a flag
Her shopping bag is lunch!

The Elephant

I'm a huge and hefty kid
And big in every way.
With ears the size of garbage lids,
I drinks tons of water each day.

Though my eyes are round and small
I see the tiniest fellow.
And when I raise my trunk to call
I give the loudest bellow.

And when an urgent call is sent
My nose will bend and sway.
You don't want to mess with elephant
It's why creatures run away.

The Anteater

The anteater wears the woolliest pants.
And dines on grubs and termite.
For desert, he selects the most succulent ants.
And gobbles it down in delight.

Lights in my Backyard Zoo

At dusk when all is still

I find creatures small.

They live in my back yard.

They fly and sometimes crawl.

In the long blades of grass,

And near the bark of trees

I search the dim lit skies,

And through the rustling leaves.

And there in my giant backyard zoo

Small creatures shine their light.

And flutter about like twinkling stars

All through the long dark night.

A Fishy School

Follow the leader.
He knows the way.
When he turns left
We'll quickly obey.
If we swim together
In a large fishy school
Sharks won't catch us.
Isn't that cool.
We'll zig and we'll zag
Deep in the water.
We'll search for some supper
Before it gets hotter.
Worms and seaweed
Are a great find.
Shhhhhh ...... did you say shark!
Let's hope he's blind.

The Cricket's Song

When all the world is dark and still

A song is sung beneath my windowsill.

The sound echoes in my head

As I lay down upon my bed.

Soon it becomes a concert sound

With crickets singing on the ground.

First, one starts, then others join in.

Sounding like out of tune violins.

The Jerboa

In the desert while he's able

The jerboa sets the table

With insect butter spread,

And crunchy seeds upon his bread.

With feet the size of two

He's a mousy kangaroo,

Wearing sandshoes on his feet,

While dancing to the beat.

Then at night when all is cool

The jerboa goes to school

And learns how not to be

An owl's snack with tea!